LIFE IN AMERICA 100 YEARS AGO

Industry and Business

LIFE IN AMERICA 100 YEARS AGO

Industry and Business

Linda Leuzzi

Chelsea House Publishers
Philadelphia

CHELSEA HOUSE PUBLISHERS
Editorial Director: Richard Rennert
Production Manager: Pamela Loos
Art Director: Sara Davis
Picture Editor: Judy Hasday

LIFE IN AMERICA 100 YEARS AGO
Senior Editor: John Ziff

Staff for *INDUSTRY AND BUSINESS*
Editorial Assistant: Kristine Brennan
Designer: Terry Mallon
Picture Researcher: Sandy Jones

First Printing

1 3 5 7 9 8 6 4 2
Library of Congress Cataloging-in-Publication Data
Leuzzi, Linda.
    Industry and business/Linda Leuzzi
    96 pp. cm. — (Life in America 100 years ago)
    Includes bibliographical references and index.
    Summary: Presents a historical overview of the development of American industry from
    post-Civil War to the twentieth century.
    ISBN 0-7910-2846-1
    1. Industries—United States—History—19th century—Juvenile literature. 2. Industries—
United States—History—20th century—Juvenile literature. 3. Inventors—United States—
History—19th century—Juvenile literature. 4. Inventors—United States—History—20th century—
Juvenile literature. 5. Trade-unions—United States—History—19th century—Juvenile literature. 6.
Trade-unions—United States—History—20th century—Juvenile literature. [1. Industries—History.
2. Inventors. 3. Labor unions—History.] I. Title II. Series.

HC105.7.L48 1997   96-45199
338.0973—dc21
CIP
AC

CONTENTS

LIFE IN AMERICA 100 YEARS AGO

Communication

Education

Frontier Life

Government and Politics

Health and Medicine

Industry and Business

Law and Order

Manners and Customs

Sports and Recreation

Transportation

Urban Life

Industry and Business

The Rise of American Industry

I get up at half-past five o'clock every morning and make myself a cup of coffee on the oil stove. I eat a bit of bread and perhaps some fruit and then go to work. I get in there soon after six o'clock so as to be in good time, tho the factory does not open till seven. At seven o'clock we all sit down to our machines and the boss brings to each one the pile of work that he or she is to finish during the day, what they call in English their "stint." Sometimes the work is not all finished by six o'clock and then the one who is behind must work overtime. The machines go like mad all day because the faster you work the more money you get. Sometimes in my haste I get my finger caught and the needle goes right through it. We all have accidents like that. Sometimes a finger has to come off.

At the turn of the century, even a living room could be converted into a sweatshop like this one, on New York's East Side. Labor contractors counted on the constant flow of immigrants, who were desperate for even the grueling, ill-paying piecework being done here.

Sixteen-year-old Sadie Frowne wrote those words at the turn of the century. Frowne, a Jewish immigrant from Poland, worked sewing garments in a sweatshop (a small, cramped factory whose workers toiled long hours for meager pay) in the Brownsville section of Brooklyn, New York. Six mornings each week, she walked to the brick factory, climbed the stairs to the third floor, and took her place at her sewing machine, one of 14 crammed into a room that measured just 20 by 14 feet. Hunched over the cotton, calico, and woolen underskirts she had to assemble, bringing her sewing machine to life by pressing her feet on a treadle, Frowne was understandably exhausted by day's end. Her pay? Five dollars and 50 cents a week.

It was the persistence and courage of industrial workers like Frowne, who tackled gritty, tough jobs day after day, that helped the United States become the world leader in quality and quantity of goods produced by 1894. The total value of American manufactured products jumped from $3 billion in 1869 to over $13 billion by the turn of the century. National wealth grew from $65 billion to $90 billion within the 1890s alone.

The evolution of the United States into an industrial power was a gradual process, though. Most of the early colonists supported themselves through farming. Land was inexpensive, and much of it was ideal for growing crops. Settlers who came to the middle colonies, for example, discovered a six-month-long growing season. That meant plenty of time to plant and harvest the grain crops they had relied on in their old countries: wheat, oats, rye, and barley.

The early farmers produced nearly everything they needed themselves, including food, clothing, furniture, barrels, tools, and even nails. When villages formed, farm women sold surplus produce for extra income or bartered it for goods and services.

11

By 1650 American colonists were hunting right whales, whose migrations took them near the New England coast, for their blubber. One hundred years later, America's whaling industry was well established, and whaleships were taking long journeys to the deep-water grounds of the sperm whale. By 1775 the whaling industry employed about 4,000 people.

A woodcut of Eli Whitney's Connecticut gun factory, circa 1830. Whitney's use of interchangeable parts in the manufacture of guns ushered in the era of mass production and heralded the end of the independent craftsperson.

The United States would remain largely agricultural from 1620 until 1860, but many industries did exist. Fishing was a major industry, especially in the Middle Atlantic and New England states. As far back as 1641—about 20 years after the Pilgrims landed at Plymouth—cod was New England's biggest product, with 300,000 of the fish exported annually. Also caught were bluefish, herring, mackerel, salmon, and shad. The fishing industry experienced steady growth, and just before the American Revolution, an estimated 10,000 people were catching fish worth a total of about $2 million. This did not include whaling, which was considered a separate industry; between 1770 and 1775, about 4,000 people worked in the whaling industry.

Once fishing boats returned to the wharves, their cargo was separated for three main uses. Fresh catches that were too large or heavy to cure for export were sold locally at the markets. (Curing involved the salting and drying of fish to preserve them.) Usually excellent-quality, smaller catches were cured, then shipped to southern Europe. Fish that were damaged, of poor quality, or too small to be cured were sent to the West Indies, where they were purchased as food for slaves or for fertilizer.

Before the Industrial Revolution, which began in England in the late 18th century, everything was made by hand. Craftspeople—including, among others, carpenters, furniture makers, silversmiths, blacksmiths, and printers—spent years learning their particular trade through a three-step process that originated in Europe. The process began with apprenticeship, during which a young worker served—and learned from—an experienced master craftsman. Apprentices received room and board but no pay. Apprenticeship might last anywhere from three to seven years, after which the person received the title of journeyman and worked for a master craftsman with pay. Eventually the journey-man could become a master craftsman and establish a business of his or her own. Masters took pride in their work—to be successful, they had to, for they got their business through recommendations from satisfied customers.

Around the time the colonists were fighting for their independence, a series of inventions was emerging in England that would dramatically change the way people worked. Perhaps the most important of these was the improved steam engine devised by the Scottish engineer James Watt. By efficiently harnessing the power of steam, the engine enabled work to be done more quickly, a key component of the modern factory system.

Changes were springing up across the Atlantic as well. After the American Revolution, mass production techniques gradually came into use in the United States. Eli Whitney cut patterns for interchangeable parts and began mass-producing muskets in his New Haven, Connecticut, factory in 1798. Whitney's guns were cheaper than hand-made counterparts, and, since the parts were interchangeable, repairs involved simply buying the necessary replacement parts rather than having them custom-made by a gunsmith.

Large, power-driven machines were gradually replacing craftspeople in the production of consumer goods, and mills and factories slowly replaced private shops. The significance of this change can hardly be overstated. In 1800 skilled craftspeople made up about 60 percent of the nation's nonfarm workers. They typically used their own tools, worked from their homes or small shops located near their homes, and, because they were in business for themselves, received the profits from their labor. Production was time-consuming (consider, for example, how long it would take to produce a single musket if all the parts—stock, barrel, hammer, trigger, trigger guard—were produced by hand), and manufactured goods were therefore relatively expensive. Production was also spread out—a large town might have a number of gunsmiths, for example, each producing a few of the muskets the townspeople bought.

With the coming of mills and factories, unskilled laborers could produce goods on a large scale in a central location. Because the machinery used in production was theirs, the mill or factory owners received all of the profits from production, paying their laborers hourly or weekly wages. Even though factory-made goods sold for less than handmade goods, the larger quantities produced meant that the factory owners' profits were potentially quite high.

The new mode of production profoundly affected ordinary people. Everyone needed clothing, for instance, but making the cloth by hand —which was often done in the home—was extremely time-consuming. Grandmother Brown, whose family settled in the small town of Athens, Ohio, in 1809, wrote about how cloth was made in her memoirs:

> My mother used to spin. She made beautiful fine thread. . . . They colored it with butternut bark. I remember too that my mother raised flax, spun it into linen, wove it into cloth, colored blue in the yarn, made it up into a dress for me which she embroidered in white above the hem. I wish I had kept that dress to show my children the beautiful work of their grandmother.

The textile industry replaced homespun material with bolts of ready-made fabrics in different weaves and colors. Samuel Slater and his associates set up the first successful textile factory in Pawtucket, Rhode Island, in 1793.

Wage work for women began in the cities, and by 1816 two out of three industrial workers were women. The Lowell mills were a logical next step.

A little girl spins fabric in a Georgia textile mill. The mill system, first established on a large scale by Francis Lowell, essentially ended the common practice of making cloth in the home.

Francis Lowell set up a mill system for the manufacture of cloth, called the Hamilton Manufacturing Company, on the banks of the Merrimack River in Lowell, Massachusetts. There canals fed the water power that ran the mills. Young, unmarried farm daughters, mostly from the New England countryside, supplied the labor. The women lived in boardinghouses—at one point there were 500 of them to house

An engraving showing steelworkers using the Bessemer process. This steelmaking technique, brought to the United States after the Civil War, revolutionized American industry by making steel available at affordable prices.

A Union Pacific construction crew, 1868. The expansion of America's railroad system after the Civil War spurred economic growth by making the transportation of goods more efficient.

the workers for Lowell's 33 mills—run by widows. They worked from 5:00 A.M. to 7:30 P.M., with half-hour meal breaks and strict curfews. Their work was varied; they might weave, spin, warp, or card wool. The pay was meager and the entire arrangement exploitive. Sarah G. Bagley, a young mill worker, received $1.75 in weekly wages; $1.25 went for room and board. But what attracted the young women was independence and intellectual stimulation unavailable on the typical farm, including public lecture series, language classes, and lending libraries.

By 1848 Lowell had become the largest industrial center in the country. Its mills wove 50,000 miles of cotton cloth each year. The large community of women working at the Lowell mills formed an unofficial labor union. In fact, they became the first group in the country to strike for better wages. Sarah Bagley helped initiate the movement for a 10-hour workday, although it didn't succeed under her leadership.

While factories vastly increased product output, they eliminated the need for special skills. Creating goods was reduced to a series of repetitive steps; in fact, many workers spent their entire day performing a single activity. The skilled craftsperson who thrived in the early 1800s was not needed by factory owners, who were able to keep wages low and thus to maximize their profits by hiring inexperienced workers. Working conditions also remained harsh.

After the Civil War, a confluence of factors fueled a tremendous growth in American industry. Large-scale immigration provided a ready work force—most of the immigrants were fleeing religious persecution or dismal economic conditions and were willing to take almost any job at whatever pay was offered. In turn, these immigrants created a market for food, clothing, and household necessities.

In addition, America's economic climate was right for business expansion. In the absence of the high tariffs and legal restrictions that stunted European trade, American manufacturers were able to sell their products in states thousands of miles away from the factories. The ever-expanding network of railroads made transporting the goods quick and economical. By 1900 approximately 193,000 miles of track were in place —a significant jump from the 35,000 miles that had been laid by 1865.

An increase in the money available for capital investment—that is, money used to buy goods (such as machinery) that are used to produce more goods—further fueled industrial development. Corporations had existed in the country since colonial times, but they emerged in the form we know them today after the Civil War, when industrialists realized that they couldn't finance their ventures alone or with a small group of investors. Affluent citizens began investing in businesses by buying stocks. If the company folded, investors might lose what their stock was worth, but they weren't liable for corporate debts. With this system in place, it was easier for entrepreneurs to raise the money they needed for new ventures.

New technologies helped advance industry as well. The steel industry is a good example. Initially, steel was used only for fine weapons and tools because it was very expensive to produce by hand. But the invention in the 1850s of the Bessemer process, which forced air through molten pig iron to extract impurities, and the introduction in 1868 of Abram S. Hewitt's open hearth process allowed steel to be made in much larger quantities and therefore more cheaply. This opened up many new markets for its use. Locomotives and rails, for example, could now be made of steel. As business boomed in various sectors of the economy, American society was gradually transformed.

The Innovators

IT WAS, SAID *SCIENTIFIC AMERICAN* MAGAZINE, "AN EPOCH of invention and progress unique in the history of the world." Between 1866 and 1896, the number of patents issued more than doubled. The pace of invention quickened as one innovation led to the possibility of—and need for—further inventions. Advances in science found applications in industry, and conversely, the needs of industry spurred science on to new discoveries. As inventors built upon and improved the work of one another, many devices and systems familiar to us today began to take shape.

Perhaps no one epitomized the spirit of this age better than Thomas Alva Edison. The Ohio-born inventor, one of history's most prolific, received over 1,000 patents for work he had personally done or had supervised at his research laboratories in Menlo Park and West Orange, New Jersey. Edison shunned research that had no clear commercial application. Instead, he concentrated on improving the inventions of others and on devising marketable products. Among his many inventions are the phonograph, an early version of the motion-picture camera, and a device for viewing moving pictures.

Thomas Edison at his Menlo Park, New Jersey, laboratory. Although best remembered for his light bulb, the prolific Edison—who applied himself only to ideas that had clear-cut commercial uses— actually had more than 1,000 patents to his credit.

The installation of an Edison dynamo (an electrical generator), July 4, 1883. Edison's first power stations served only a handful of customers, but the dream of bringing electricity into every home spawned a huge power industry and forever altered Americans' way of life.

But Edison's most important contribution was his invention of an improved incandescent light and a practical system for supplying electricity to make it work. In essence, he laid the foundations for something we take completely for granted: the use of electricity in our houses, schools, businesses, and public places.

The idea for the light bulb did not originate with Edison. Dating back to 1802, more than 20 others from Engand, France, Russia, Canada, and America had worked on the light bulb. And at the same time that Edison was conducting his experiments, there were three or four other inventors from England and France as well as Hiram S. Maxim, a serious rival from the United States, who had created working incandescent lamps.

What set Edison apart was his vision. His incandescent lamp, which he patented in 1879, was the first step in the development of the huge electrical system that would produce, distribute, and control this energy. Edison dreamed of bringing electricity right into people's homes via underground wires and generators. No one else had considered this possibility.

At the time, electric lighting did exist in the form of arc lighting, a very powerful illumination fueled by generators that was used for lighthouses and public areas. But, at 4,000 candlepower (that is, roughly as bright as 4,000 candles), it was much too overpowering for use in the home. (Gaslight, which was widely used in homes, had 10-to-20-candlepower illumination.) With Wall Street backing for research and development, Edison pursued his dream doggedly. When someone commented on his godlike genius, Edison shouted, "Godlike nothing! Sticking to it is the genius."

By 1882 Edison had opened his first commercial power station in New York City. It served approximately 85 customers and lit a mere 400 lamps. But before the turn of the century, 2,774 power stations were operating, and the effects on people's lives were enormous. Grandma Brown, who lived to be 100 and saw the 19th century unfold, summed up electricity's impact. "If one wants light now," she explained, "all one has to do is pull a string or push a button. Then we had to pick up a coal with tongs, hold it against a candle, and blow. And one had to make the candles, perhaps."

Although Edison had revolutionized American life, he hadn't thought of everything. His incandescent lights, ingenious as they were, burned out quickly. They lasted for only about two nights and a day.

In 1882 an African American by the name of Lewis Howard Latimer patented a method that made the light bulb burn longer. Latimer mounted carbon filaments to the lead wires at the base of the lamp (carbonized-cotton sewing threads had been used in earlier lamps). Then he surrounded these carbon filaments with thin cardboard casings, giving them firmness and shape.

Latimer achieved his accomplishments through a combination of talent and sheer will. A bright student, he had to drop out of school when he was 10 to help support his family. Later on, he rose from office boy to head draftsman at Crosby and Gould, a Boston law firm that specialized in patent applications, by teaching himself how to draw. Interestingly, Latimer worked with Alexander Graham Bell on the drawing for Bell's telephone patent. It was from Bell that he learned about electricity.

Eventually, Latimer joined with Hiram Maxim, Edison's rival. Maxim was impressed with Latimer's drafting expertise and hired him as an assistant manager and draftsman for his company, U.S. Electric.

28

When Alexander Graham Bell spilled some of the acid from his liquid phone onto his clothes, he called for his assistant. "Mr. Watson, come here; I want you," Bell said into the transmitter. The date was March 10, 1876, and that seemingly routine utterance went down in history as the first ever heard clearly over an electric telephone. The liquid phone's transmission device is the tall object on the table.

Had fate turned even slightly against Alexander Graham Bell (shown here opening the New York–Chicago telephone line), he would have been a historical footnote. On February 14, 1876, Bell beat rival inventor Elisha Gray to the patent office with his plans for the telephone by a mere two hours.

Maxim needed someone to produce U.S. patent drawings; he was also involved in a fierce patent war with Edison for the rights to the incandescent light.

As an employee of U.S. Electric, Latimer perfected the shape and structure of the cardboard filaments, filed for the patent, then turned it over to the company. Maxim put Latimer in charge of overseeing the installation of lighting systems for numerous buildings.

Edison, who discovered Latimer's skills during his patent fight with Maxim, tapped him to work at the Edison Electric Company on Fifth Avenue in Manhattan in 1884. Latimer would become a key Edison aide, serving as chief draftsman and expert witness for Edison Electric's patent board.

Another invention that would have a profound impact on modern society was the telephone. Though the name of Alexander Graham Bell is forever linked with this device, in early 1876 Bell was racing with another inventor, Elisha Gray, to patent a system for transmitting the voice electrically. In fact, on February 14 Bell submitted his invention to the patent office just two hours before Gray submitted plans for a rival system. Bell's prototype would not have worked because the transmitter was flawed, but he came up with an improved version later on. Despite the fact that Gray's original plans *were* sound, Bell was awarded the patent.

Like Edison, Bell had a talent for the bigger picture—and he had a lifelong interest in the mechanics of sound and speech. As youngsters, he and his brother experimented with artificial vocal cords. Later he taught "visible speech," a method his father had invented for teaching the deaf to speak. There's no doubt that Bell's background helped set the foundation for his success.

By 1844 the telegraph had emerged as a practical method of long-distance communication, and thousands of miles of wire were strung up across the country. Messages were sent over the wires in Morse code (a system using patterns of long and short signals to represent letters) via a transmitter and a receiver. As revolutionary as this electrical mode of communication was, the telegraph had some drawbacks. Only one message per wire could be sent or received at a time. In a large, bustling city, with thousands of people and businesses, either a vast number of lines would have to be constructed or messages would frequently be delayed.

Bell began working on a way to send multiple messages simultaneously over the same line. The key, he believed, lay in the work of the German physicist Hermann von Helmholz. Von Helmholz had joined an electromagnet with a tuning fork and had found that by quickly pulling the fork he could send an electric current through the wire if it vibrated at the same frequency—that is, the same number of sound waves per second—as the tuning fork. Bell felt that the answer to the problem of sending multiple telegraph messages was to hook up several tuning forks to a wire. Each tuning fork could carry a different signal if he could figure out how to separate one signal from the other. To do this, Bell devised a set of receiving reeds, each one an exact match in frequency with one of the forks. Bell's initial device was called a harmonic telegraph.

The idea for the telephone emerged during Bell's painstaking telegraph experiments in a small workroom on Court Street in Boston. While working with James Watson, a gifted mechanic, Bell heard a distinct, electrically transmitted noise. For years, Bell had thought about the idea that speech could be carried through the wires, and he had seen a device called a telephone in experiments by Johann Philip Reiss in 1861 at the Massachusetts Institute of Technology. The idea fascinated him. When he heard the sound that Watson inadvertently made over the wire, Bell and his partner worked on a mouthpiece.

Investors had to be convinced that this new invention wasn't a toy (essentially the approach Elisha Gray took), but through Bell's perseverance, commercial telephone service began in 1877. Almost half a million telephones were installed by the American Telegraph and Telephone Company in cities nationwide by the 1890s, and talking to someone in a different city became routine.

Although history books tend to focus on the achievements of male inventors during this period, women made significant contributions that changed the course of business as well as everyday life. In fact, as of March 15, 1895, the patent commissioner listed a total of 5,535 women inventors since the office's establishment in 1790.

Vacuum packing, a process still used today, was invented by Amanda Theodosia Jones in 1873. Canning had been around for a while; but her unique "Jones process" expelled the air from cans or bottles at a high temperature, laying the groundwork for the pure food industry. Jones had been a teacher and a journalist before setting her sights on invention and had never canned food before beginning her experiments. But after studying and mastering the process, she applied for and received several patents and raised $1 million in capital for the Woman's Canning and Preserving Company in Chicago, where just about all the officers and employees were women. By 1895 Jones's enterprise was cranking out 200,000 cans of food annually.

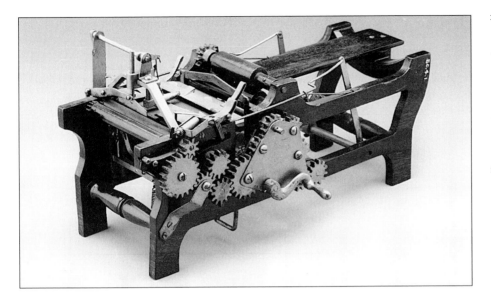

Margaret Knight's machine for making paper bags, patented in 1870. A former child mill worker, Knight made a fortune from her inventions and was called "a woman Edison."

The U.S. Navy, members of Congress, and shipping masters and their crewmen were among those who praised Martha Coston's pyrotechnic night signal, a holder for different color-coded explosives that ignited when twisted, enabling ships to communicate. We know them today as flares. Coston was a widow with four small children who for years searched for the right combination of chemicals to produce the signals. Her patents in the United States and abroad made her a fortune.

Just about every American has used paper bags. Margaret Knight of Springfield, Massachusetts, patented a machine that produced square-bottom bags in 1870. Before Knight's invention, most of the assembly was done by hand. Knight's machine did the work of 30 people and was a sensation when introduced in this country and in Europe. The feisty inventor, who had been a child mill worker, shot to fame and prosperity.

35

Knight had little schooling but was a natural with machines. She was an employee of the Columbia Paper Bag Company, running machinery and making a third less than her male colleagues, when she decided to patent her idea. It wasn't an easy road. After someone tried to steal the idea, Knight brought a patent interference suit, which she eventually won. Along with a Newton, Massachusetts, businessman she then formed the Eastern Paper Bag Company of Hartford, Connecticut, receiving a lucrative deal that included royalties, company stocks, and dividends.

During her lifetime, Knight received 14 patents for various inventions; the last, in 1912, came two years before her death, when she was well into her 70s and was called "a woman Edison" by the *Framingham Evening News*.

The inventions of people like Edison, Bell, and Knight not only offered the possibility of an improved quality of life for everyone, but they also fueled the profits of American business and industry. As the 19th century came to a close, these profits increasingly became concentrated in the hands of a few.

Financeers and Industrialists

A 1,340-FOOT-LONG WOODEN WALL, CONSTRUCTED BY Governor Peter Stuyvesant in 1643 for the protection of Manhattan's Dutch colonists, gave Wall Street, the world's most famous financial center, its name. In the beginning, the area was a draw for pirates—Captain Kidd, for example, lived at 56 Wall Street. But by the early 18th century, merchants had moved in, and the sound of public auctions became a regular part of street activity.

Coffee houses popped up, and they became the new gathering places for the auctions, which began to include stocks and bonds. While many of these establishments were destroyed during the revolutionary war, those that survived counted among their patrons senators and congressmen (New York City was the country's capital) as well as traders and brokers. These wealthy and influential men shared their economic and business views in the relaxed setting, forging an informal partnership between business and government.

Wall Street, America's financial heart, as it looked in 1880. With buildings rising skyward on both sides, the narrow street depicted here is already the arena of bustling activity that we know today.

By the end of the 18th century, the rudiments of the modern stock exchange were in place. Someone who wanted to sell his or her stocks and bonds would contact an auctioneer, who would announce the upcoming sale. Interested buyers would gather at the auctioneer's table on Wall Street and bid. Stocks and bonds in banks, insurance companies, dock and road construction, and mining companies could be bought and sold.

Banks became part of the American financial world in 1781, when the Bank of North America was founded in Philadelphia. By 1801 the country had 23 chartered banks, which frequently joined with insurance companies in business ventures. The bank would lend money to a businessperson and the insurance company would in turn finance the bank loan by floating notes, written promises to pay debts.

Production of iron ore, lumber, and petroleum soared during the Civil War, but the wealth generated by the railroads was truly mind-boggling. Because troops and war supplies had to be transported virtually nonstop, freight doubled in volume. As the railroad companies' earnings skyrocketed, shareholders saw the value of their stocks go through the roof and collected hefty dividends. The Hudson River Railroad's stock, for example, shot from $31 a share to $164 a share.

Owners and investors put much of their profits into savings, thereby benefiting the banks as well. Depositors enjoyed interest rates ranging from a minimum of 7 percent to an average of between 10 and 15 percent; one bank paid as high as 24 percent.

Many people profited from the Civil War, and not always by honest means. For example, contractors often supplied the federal government with inferior-quality goods, pocketing the money they saved on material and production costs. But such conduct amounted to more than simply

Traders check the results of a day's session at the New York Stock Exchange in 1905. The late 19th and early 20th centuries saw a rise in the number of millionaires who made their fortunes in the stock market.

Wall Street speculator Jay Gould used his tremendous wealth to exert control over telegraph companies, the press, and especially —as this 1885 political cartoon suggests—the New York legal system. He siphoned huge bribes into that state's legislature in exchange for tacit permission to continue his illegal business practices without interference.

bilking the government; it sometimes had dire consequences for the soldiers of the Union army. Guns blew up in soldiers' faces. Some Union uniforms, initially blue, quickly faded to gray, causing their unfortunate wearers to be mistaken for Confederate soldiers. Wool blankets made from cheap, thin material were almost useless on cold nights.

According to the *New York Independent*, there were only 20 people in the entire country before 1850 with a personal net worth of $1 million; by 1863 there were several hundred millionaires, some worth up to $20 million, in New York City alone. By 1892 there were 4,000 millionaires in the United States. While the average industrialist enjoyed modest success, a new class emerged that accumulated huge fortunes and exercised great control over American industry by the early 1900s.

Jay Gould is a case in point. A Wall Street speculator, he began buying railroad shares at the start of the Civil War, purchasing the stock low, then selling it high. It was rumored that he knew when the troops and shipments were being moved—a tremendous business advantage— because he bribed the War Office. In 1868 Gould and Jim Fisk, directors of the Erie Railroad, fought to prevent shipping and railroad magnate Cornelius Vanderbilt from acquiring the Erie. To do this, they illegally released 100,000 new Erie shares onto the market, making a fortune in the process. Gould then paid $100,000 in bribes to members of the New York legislature, which subsequently voted to block Vanderbilt's takeover attempt. (Unfortunately for Vanderbilt, he had given the legislature only $75,000.)

This sort of dishonesty was fairly common in American business and industry of the era, and most industrialists didn't care what the public thought. In this respect, Gould was an exception; he cultivated an image of concern for the financial well-being of others.

When the publisher of the *New York Tribune* needed money to keep the paper in business, Gould lent him the funds and in return received a controlling interest in the paper. Gould also invested heavily in the *New York World*. He used this financial leverage to influence editorial writing, and the management of companies he wanted to take over was always portrayed as incompetent or worse. Although he once said, "I can hire one half of the working class to kill the other half," Gould's takeovers were always depicted as beneficial to the stockholders, whom he was saving from a badly run company.

James Buchanan Duke, who headed the American Tobacco Company, summed up big business tactics. "First you hit your enemies in the pocketbook, hit 'em hard. Then you either buy 'em out or take 'em in with you." What he was talking about was consolidation, and cartels were the earliest forms. Pools of independent business firms in the same field would agree to charge the same prices and avoid competitive price cutting. This succeeded in keeping profits high until recessions hit. Also, the verbal agreements that formed the basis of most cartels were basically unenforceable.

When cartels could no longer guarantee profits, trusts—huge corporations that attempted to gain control of entire markets by merging with or swallowing up all competitors—evolved. The first, the Standard Oil Trust, was formed in 1882. John D. Rockefeller, who headed the Standard Oil Company of Ohio, had already purchased 80 percent of the oil refineries in Cleveland as well as refineries in other major cities. By 1879 his massive company controlled over 90 percent of the nation's refining capacity and also dominated nearly every aspect of the storage and transportation of oil. To administer this giant empire, Rockefeller formed the trust, whose hold on America's petroleum industry ensured huge profits.

In this 1905 cartoon, John D. Rockefeller's competitors are unwanted buds that the oil magnate has pruned away to enable his Standard Oil flower (profits) to blossom luxuriantly.

Steel magnate Andrew Carnegie donated staggering amounts of money for the public good, yet he could be quite ruthless in his dealings with labor. Carnegie's determination to rid his Homestead steel plant of the Amalgamated Association of Iron and Steel Workers union led to a bloody showdown between strikers and Pinkerton agents hired to protect replacement workers.

A decade after the formation of the Standard Oil Trust, however, the Ohio Supreme Court ordered it dissolved. In 1899 Rockefeller relocated to New Jersey, where incorporation laws permitted the existence of holding companies (companies whose function is to hold a controlling interest in the stocks of other companies). Most of the companies that made up the Standard Oil Trust joined the Standard Oil Company of New Jersey, so in effect the holding company kept Rockefeller's vast petroleum empire intact. (It wasn't until 1911 that Standard Oil of New Jersey was finally dissolved following a decision by the U.S. Supreme Court.)

As John D. Rockefeller was consolidating his hold on American oil production, Andrew Carnegie was transforming America's steel industry. The Scottish-born Carnegie has been celebrated for his philanthropy—indeed, he gave away staggering sums of money during his lifetime—but the business practices he used to amass his fortune were as self-serving as anyone else's. Carnegie once explained how industrial power worked: If he wanted great contracts for steel rails, he was able to get them because he was friends with the presidents of railroads like the Union Pacific and the Southern Pacific. Carnegie also extended credit at times, which meant that he received favors in return. Smaller competitors, no matter how smart, hardworking, or inventive, didn't have the resources to offer credit.

Around the end of the Civil War, Carnegie invested in an iron works and was soon making handsome profits. A few years later, while on a trip to England, he became acquainted with the Bessemer process for making steel. He returned to the United States convinced that a fortune could be made in the steel industry, and he proceeded to prove it. He built the J. Edgar Thomson steel mill near Pittsburgh and, while the rest of American industry struggled through an economic depression in the 1870s, expanded his Carnegie Steel Company tremendously. By 1890 Carnegie had an income of $2 million a year and was worth $30 million.

A large part of Carnegie's success lay in his emphasis on cost cutting; he kept salaries down and used machines instead of workers whenever possible. Throughout the 25 years he spent building his fortune in the steel business, he reviewed company costs every week without fail. He examined virtually every cent that was spent. Ever on the lookout for money-saving tactics, Carnegie didn't renew fire insurance after discovering it was cheaper to replace the company's wooden buildings with iron ones.

Carnegie also recognized the importance of putting a percentage of his profits back into the business. He knew that staying on top meant keeping up with the latest technology, so he reinvested in each new advance as it became available. He acquired the Pittsburgh Bessemer Steel Company's Homestead works in large part because he wanted its state-of-the-art equipment. Unfortunately for Carnegie, Homestead also had labor troubles.

Part of Carnegie's genius was his ability to find talented people for key positions in his company. "Captain" Bill Jones had worked for him since the 1870s. Jones managed the workers at all of Carnegie's plants, showing particular skill in handling management problems and avoiding disputes. Just as important, though, he respected the employees. But Jones died in a furnace explosion in 1889 and was replaced by Henry Clay Frick—tough, uncompromising, and antilabor.

By the early 1890s the most powerful union in the country was the Amalgamated Association of Iron and Steel Workers, which had a

(continued on page 54)

A family works together in a turn-of-the-century New York sweatshop.

"Uncle Sam removing the unholy operators." This 1881 cartoon depicts the government's breakup of the telegraph monopoly held by Jay Gould and Cornelius Vanderbilt.

Weary steel workers rest during their lunch break. Painting by Thomas P. Anshutz, ca. 1890.

A scene from the Chicago Stock Exchange. Trading wasn't as regulated as it is today, and some investors made fortunes through questionable practices.

A drawing of the 1892 Homestead strike conveys the large scale, heated passions, and violence of the conflict.

(continued from page 48)

strong presence at the Homestead plant. The Amalgamated's members were skilled and influential, and they had won some major victories in the area of working conditions. Both Carnegie and Frick wanted the Amalgamated out. In 1892, when the old contract was up, the Amalgamated was kept out of negotiations—a major insult, as it had been included in the past as a bargaining agent.

Carnegie took off for Scotland and let Frick handle the situation. It was Frick's intention to force a confrontation. Sliding-scale wages (wages linked to the selling price of the product) were again reduced with the intent of goading the workers to strike, and they did. Frick even had barbed wire strung around the steel works and watchtowers with rifle slits constructed in preparation for a struggle. The plan was to hire Pinkerton guards to protect the company when the plant opened its doors to nonunion workers.

What Frick didn't count on was the anger of the union workers and the people who lived in the area. The Pinkerton guards, who were to be smuggled in on barges at night, were spotted. They couldn't leave the barges because the strikers and townspeople attacked them ferociously from the riverbank, firing guns and hurling anything they could get their hands on. A truce was negotiated, but the Pinkertons still had to pass through a raging mob. Several guards and strikers were killed. When the company asked for militia protection, Pennsylvania's governor sent 8,000 National Guard troops to the site to protect the strikebreakers. Frick was shot by a radical, but not fatally; he reopened Homestead.

Four months later, the Amalgamated gave in to the company's demands. Upon hearing of the union's capitulation, Carnegie, who didn't want to be blamed for the tragic situation, wired Frick from Europe, "Life is worth living again."

Carnegie had shown his hypocritical side, and the nation's press went after him. "Three months ago Andrew Carnegie was a man to be envied. Today he is an object of mingled pity and contempt," said the *St. Louis Dispatch.*

> A single word from him might have saved the bloodshed—but the word was never spoken. Nor has he, from that bloody day until this, said anything except that he had "implicit confidence in the managers of the mills." Ten thousand "Carnegie Public Libraries" would not compensate the country for the direct and indirect evils resulting from the Homestead lockout.

Carnegie was crushed by the negative publicity; this was a man who wrote magazine articles in favor of labor. But he kept building his empire until 1900, when he sold his company to Charles Schwab. He received $350 million in stocks from the sale and became the richest man in the world.

To Carnegie's credit, he did give away every penny he made in the sale to Schwab. But he was one of the industrialists who paved the way for monopolies. By 1904 roughly 40 percent of the country's industrial goods were produced by about 2,000 of the nation's largest firms.

The Workers

BY 1900 THERE WERE 76 MILLION PEOPLE LIVING IN THE continental United States, 19 million of whom were in the work force. The economy had been growing more diversified, and with this came an increased variety of occupations along with an emerging middle class. The 1890 census listed 61 different occupations under categories such as agricultural pursuits, professional service, domestic and personal service, trade and transportation, manufacturing, and mechanical pursuits. These occupations included farm owner, actor, musician, surgeon, restauranteur, police officer, banker, accountant, bookbinder, cabinetmaker, and wheelwright.

The increasing complexity of the economy led to a need for workers with specialized knowledge and skills. Colleges—many built during the Civil War era thanks in part to the 1862 Morrill Land Grant Act, which gave federal land to states for the establishment of institutions of higher learning—helped fill this need. By the end of the century, 69 new colleges had been founded.

The administration building at Howard University, Washington, D.C. As the 19th century gave way to the 20th, colleges and trade schools sprang up to train workers for the specialized jobs created by industrialization. As a black institution, Howard University had a dual mission: to develop its students' marketable skills and to help stamp out racial inequality in a country that had, until recently, condoned slavery.

In addition, some of the wealthy industrialists, recognizing the need for specialized skills in the workplace, gave generously to existing institutions and occasionally funded new ones. Architecture, engineering, business, journalism, and education schools were added to colleges and universities. Graduate study was also expanded: in 1875 there were only 399 graduate students; by 1900 that number had risen to 5,000. As education increased, so did salaries; pay for white-collar workers—clerks, accountants, doctors, lawyers, and other professionals—rose by one-third between 1890 and 1910.

Although numerous success stories could be found, there were also many stories of hardship for laborers. Pay was generally low, and many workers faced horrendous working conditions—mines and mills that were poorly lit and ventilated and workdays that lasted for 10 to 12 hours.

Unfortunately, the New York sweatshop conditions that Sadie Frowne wrote about existed nationwide. Florence Kelly, the nation's first state factory inspector, commented on sweatshop conditions in Illinois in 1895:

It is preposterous, on the face of it, that a trade employing from 25,000 to 30,000 persons in a single city, with an annual output of many millions of dollars, should be carried on with the same primitive machines which were used thirty years ago. . . . Everywhere steam, electricity, and human ingenuity have been pressed into service for the purpose of organization and centralization; but in the garment trades this process has been reversed, and the division of labor has [been] made a means of demoralization, disorganization, and degradation, carried to a point beyond which it is impossible to go.

Tobacco workers in Virginia around the turn of the century. The tobacco industry needed plenty of workers to perform tasks that were often tedious, as suggested by the faces of these men. Many of the most underpaid workers in the least powerful positions were black.

The problems workers faced tended to be magnified for African Americans. As racism and discrimination defined their social standing, it also limited their economic opportunities. Nevertheless, blacks found ways to prosper. For example, because the Jim Crow laws that were enacted in the South beginning in the 1880s greatly segregated the races, African Americans established businesses that served and were supported by their own community. Montgomery, Alabama, for instance, had just 2,000 African-American residents in 1900 but was home to many thriving black businesses, including 23 grocery stores, three drugstores, 12 contractors and builders, 30 shoemakers, 15 blacksmith shops, and butchers, physicians, and undertakers.

A few African Americans were able to turn their businesses into fortunes, an accomplishment that was difficult for entrepreneurs of any race. John Merrick was a former slave who taught himself to read and write. Between jobs as a barber and shoe shiner, he studied high finance. By 1892 his properties included five barbershops in Durham, North Carolina. In 1898 Merrick invested in the North Carolina Mutual and Provident Association, an insurance company. Approximately two decades after he started his insurance venture, which was renamed North Carolina Mutual Life, Merrick had built up over $16 million in the industry.

Maggie Lena was another example. Lena, the first female bank president in the United States, was a black woman who founded the St. Luke Penny Savings Bank in Richmond, Virginia, in 1903. St. Luke Penny Savings Bank eventually became the Consolidated Bank and Trust Company, and Lena served as its president until 1930.

Such success stories aside, if you were to compare America's work force 100 years ago with its work force today, you'd find a much smaller percentage of African Americans in the higher-paying professional fields. For example, by 1900 black leader Booker T. Washington counted just 350 doctors in the National Medical Association, a black organization. According to Washington, African-American women accounted for 160 physicians, 164 ministers, almost 1,200 musicians and music teachers, and 13,525 teachers.

Similarly, while women of all races made up a significant portion of the work force, they were vastly underrepresented in the professional fields. There were, of course, some who shone in "untraditional" occupations. Louise Blanchard Bethune is one example. Bethune, the country's first professional woman architect, established her own firm in 1881 and had a thriving business that designed public schools, a woman's penitentiary and an armory, and industrial and commercial buildings. She also designed the Hotel Lafayette, a 265-room, fireproof hotel in Buffalo, New York, which opened in 1904. Henriett Chamberlain King, another good example, was saddled with $500,000 in debts and the biggest ranch in Texas when her husband died in 1885. Using her business savvy, King managed her ranch, now known as the King Ranch, successfully for the next 40 years, doubling the property and building an estate worth $5 million.

America's work force of 100 years ago differed in another major respect from today's: it included a large number of young children, many of whom worked under dangerous and exploitative conditions. By 1906 there were about 2 million youths in the work force.

The expectation that children would do all sorts of chores on the family farm had been an unquestioned part of life since colonial times; it was the only way many families could survive. But as the country shifted from a predominantly agricultural economy toward an industrial one, more and more children began working in factories, frequently to the exclusion of schooling and what we now consider a normal childhood.

This photograph by Lewis Hine shows women and children processing string beans in a crowded plant under the watchful eye of their supervisor. At the turn of the century, factory owners were well aware that if they paid male workers poorly, then they could pay women and children less still.

In the early part of the 20th century, 10 percent of all girls and 20 percent of all boys aged 10 to 15 were working 12-hour days in the factories or the fields to help bring in income for their families.

Some children worked as "breaker boys," removing shards of slate among piles of coal. The coal produced a thick, dusty film that made it hard to see and coated the children's clothes and skin. In canneries, fruits and vegetables were cut up by little girls who worked 16-hour days. Understandably, the children became exhausted, and accidents—sometimes fatal—were relatively common, especially when children operated machinery.

Adults could strike, but America's child laborers were basically defenseless. Appalled by the exploitation, some reformers set out to change the situation. The first step was to document the abuses going on. Lewis Hine had been working as a freelance photographer for the National Child Labor Committee for several years before he was formally hired in 1910 as a full-time agent to photograph child labor conditions. Hine, a former teacher, related well to children. His photos captured their dignity, wisdom, wiliness, and vulnerability, and they made people think.

In "Night: City of Brotherly Love," a photo leaflet, Hine chronicled the lives of Philadelphia messengers, newsboys, and street vendors under the age of 12 who worked from 8 P.M. to 4 A.M. One photo shows a young boy, who will be "ten at Easter," holding a large stack of papers. The boy, neatly dressed in cap and knickers, looks weary; his shift isn't over until early morning and he has three hours to go. Hine's photographic skill and accompanying text chronicling the young workers of America would eventually become famous.

The photography of Lewis Hine called public attention to—and evoked strong feelings against—the exploitation of child laborers. This 1908 photo of a young Massachusetts textile worker captures the weary nobility of a child accustomed to long hours, low pay, and dangerous conditions.

In the beginning, factories cooperated with Hine's requests to photograph and interview youngsters, but over the years, resistance to the National Child Labor Committee's activities grew. When a formal request no longer worked, Hine had to find other ways to gain entry into factories. He became adept at various bluffs. Sometimes he was a Bible salesman, his camera concealed in a suitcase supposedly full of New Testament texts. Sometimes he was an insurance or postcard salesman. In these cases he could, during pauses in conversation with factory managers, glimpse into the next room where the children were working and guess the number and ages of the children employed. Sometimes he posed as an industrial photographer and asked permission to take photos of the machinery.

Once inside a factory, Hine casually spoke to the youngsters, asking about such things as their work hours and weekly pay. When these ploys didn't work, he'd set up his equipment outside the entrance of a plant, photographing and interviewing the children as they left work.

In one year alone, Hine covered more than 50,000 miles in his work for the National Child Labor Committee. He documented the child worker in mines and canneries, factories, farms, and sweatshops for 12 years. But not until 1916 was the first federal law regulating child labor passed. This law made it illegal to ship goods produced by underage children across state lines, but the law was later repealed, and child labor wasn't abolished until the 1930s.

Men and women sewing garments in a cramped sweatshop. The pay for such jobs was low, the hours long, and the working conditions difficult, but the steady stream of immigrants to the United States ensured that employers would have sufficient numbers of workers.

This 1888 woodcut depicts a young worker being chastised by a supervisor. At the time, rules protecting the rights of workers were virtually nonexistent.

Like moths drawn to a candle, investors out to make a tidy profit sometimes got burned by Wall Street financeer Jay Gould (depicted here). Gould was not above illegally releasing worthless stock onto the market, a tactic he used in 1868 to successfully fend off Cornelius Vanderbilt's attempt to acquire the Erie Railroad.

This engraving captures the desperate squalor of a tenement house sweatshop, where a single room often served as work area, kitchen, and sleeping quarters for several families.

The Unions

"I HAVE AS YET NEVER BOASTED OF WHAT I HAVE DONE IN the interest of organized labor," wrote Richard Davis, a coal miner, in 1898, "but will venture to say that I have done all I could and am proud that I am alive today, for I think I have had the unpleasant privilege of going into the most dangerous places in this country to organize, or in other words, to do the almost impossible."

For Davis, "the almost impossible" was to get miners to join a labor union, an organization that represents working men and women before their employers in matters of wages, benefits, and working conditions. As discussed earlier, industrialization brought enormous changes for the American worker. The independent craftsman was largely replaced by the wage worker, who frequently toiled long hours for low pay in unsafe or oppressive conditions. Individual workers were powerless to improve their situations: employers could simply fire anyone who complained. But if a large group of workers banded together, employers would presumably have to pay more attention to their grievances.

A tent camp of striking coal miners at Red Jacket, West Virginia. The houses that miners rented from company owners — often at exorbitant rates — were not necessarily better than the tents.

This drawing depicts the 10th annual convention of the Knights of Labor, the first national labor organization in the United States. The organization was founded in 1869.

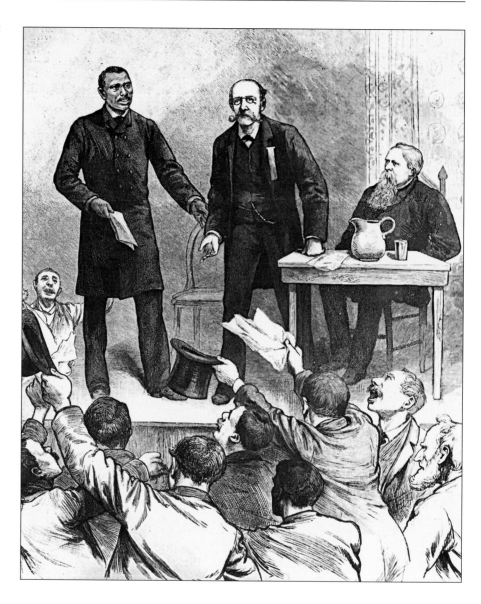

Still, unions often found it difficult to recruit members. Industrialists did their best to limit organizers' access to their workers. Plus, many workers feared that if they were seen as troublemakers, their employers would simply replace them—union or no union. And, thanks in part to the large-scale immigration that occurred in the 19th century, there was no shortage of unskilled laborers willing to accept virtually any job.

Davis, an African American who grew up in the hardscrabble village of Rendville, Ohio, spent 16 years in the labor movement and helped organize the United Mine Workers (UMW) in the 1890s. It was a tough decade for the union. Compounding the dangerous working conditions, frequent wage cuts, and recurring unemployment that miners typically faced was an economic depression that put many of them out of work for extended periods.

In 1896 and 1897 Davis was elected to the National Executive Board of the UMW. He traveled throughout Ohio and to other mining states, including Alabama and West Virginia, speaking in halls and at outdoor gatherings, attempting to organize the miners against all odds. Davis also exposed unfair labor practices—practices that illustrate why unions were needed in the first place. In Congo, Ohio, for example, mine operators promoted house-lease arrangements, company-owned houses that had to be vacated within five days if the miners went on strike or quit. The housing was also segregated. To Davis, more than the segregation resembled slavery: the fenced, gated community gave the company control over everything its residents did. "Do you see the point?" he wrote. "To keep peddling wagons out. You see they don't want the honest farmer to come in and sell his produce to the miners; no, for that would be competition and the company would not reap the profits accruing to it." Thanks to Davis's efforts, the Congo company finally recognized the union after years of resistance, cooperated on grievances, and offered small benefits.

Because of his union activities, Davis was blacklisted (denied work) by mine owners, and he knew poverty well. He died of lung disease in 1900 at age 35. But he lived to see a major victory: in 1897 mine owners in western Pennsylvania, Ohio, Indiana, and Illinois were forced to recognize the UMW.

After a bitter strike in 1902, the UMW won a 10 percent raise and a nine-hour workday. It was the efforts of people like Davis that laid the groundwork for better pay and working conditions for the country's working men and women.

The first major attempt at a national labor organization had taken place in 1869 when the Noble Order of the Knights of Labor was formed. The union included all types of workers. In 1881 women were admitted, and 192 women's assemblies were eventually established. Membership in the Knights of Labor swelled to 700,000 in 1886, but the union fizzled in the 1890s.

The Knights of Labor's rival organization at this time was the American Federation of Labor (AFL). Samuel Gompers became its first president in 1886 and held that position, except for a one-year interruption, until 1924. Gompers was realistic about American business. He knew that the capitalists were here to stay and would continue to reap the lion's share of the profits of industrial production. What he pushed for were the basic needs of the worker: fair pay, safe working conditions, and reasonable hours. Gompers was not a radical; collective bargaining —that is, negotiations between the employer and the union representative on wages, hours, and working conditions—was his approach. But if management failed to bargain in good faith, he felt that labor had a right to strike.

Samuel Gompers, the first president of the American Federation of Labor. During his 37 years in office, Gompers championed the worker's right to fair pay, decent working conditions, and reasonable hours.

Two members of the Ladies Tailors Union on strike in 1910. Another organization formed around this time, the International Ladies Garment Workers Union, remains visible and vocal today.

The AFL acted as an umbrella organization of local, skilled-craft unions, which included building trades, printing trades, metal industries, brewers, and coal miners. For example, the Amalgamated Association of Iron and Steel Workers, the group involved in the Homestead plant of the Carnegie Steel Company, was an affiliate of the AFL.

The AFL originally did not admit semiskilled or unskilled workers. Nor were blacks or women welcome. But middle-class working reformers joined with working women at the Chicago headquarters of the National Women's Trade Union in 1903; one of the union activists, Mary Anderson, later became the first director of the Women's Bureau of the U.S. Department of Labor. Anderson and other female union activists proved just as tough as their male counterparts in fighting for workers' rights. Clara Lemlich, an immigrant who fled the Russian pogroms (massacres of Jews) at age 15, became a founding member of the International Ladies Garment Workers Union in 1906 at age 18. The fiery Lemlich was arrested 17 times in one year for her role in walkouts, and she once stirred 2,000 women to strike after an impassioned speech in Yiddish. The International Ladies Garment Workers Union had successful strikes in 1909 and 1910 and achieved significant gains. Mary Harris Jones, who became better known as Mother Jones, organized coal miners in West Virginia and Colorado as well as railroad workers; she, too, was jailed for her union activities.

Despite the courage of their leaders and the determination of their members, unions experienced as many defeats as victories in their early struggles with industrialists. But they did succeed in one critical respect: they stirred the country's conscience. As early as 1886, President Rutherford B. Hayes wrote:

I agree that Labor does not get its fair share of the wealth it creates. The Sermon on the Mount, the golden rule, the Declaration of Independence all require extensive reforms to the end that labor may be so rewarded that the working man can with temperance, industry and thrift own a home, educate his children and lay up support for old age.

Mark Hanna, a powerful Republican leader and successful business-man, also spoke out for workers' rights. "A man who won't meet his men half-way," he declared, "is a God-damn fool!" One such "fool" who drew Hanna's criticism was George Pullman, owner of the Pullman Palace Car Company, which made railroad cars. During the winter of 1893–94, Pullman cut his workers' wages by an average of 25 percent while refusing to reduce rents for employee housing. This provoked a strike at Pullman's plant that soon took on national significance when the American Railway Union boycotted Pullman cars and the railroad owners retaliated by firing union members. The union then struck the railroads, and federal troops had to be dispatched to keep the trains running.

As was the case with the Pullman strike, when the government intervened in labor disputes it generally took the side of industry. But Mark Hanna felt that the unions should be recognized as legitimate organizations and was part of the National Civic Federation, founded in 1901. Joining him at the federation, which sought to foster the peaceful acceptance of collective bargaining with industry, were Samuel Gompers, John D. Rockefeller, and John Mitchell, president of the United Mine Workers.

The grandmotherly appearance of Mary Harris Jones, better known as Mother Jones, belied her toughness as a union organizer for coal miners and railroad workers. Mother Jones toiled tirelessly on behalf of labor despite being jailed for her activities.

In 1895 there were 1,400 industrial strikes involving some 700,000 workers. Despite this increased activism, union membership was rising very slowly at the turn of the century; fewer than one million workers belonged to unions in 1900. But the labor movement soon began to gain momentum. Between 1900 and 1914 the AFL grew from 550,000 members to over 2 million. During this same period, membership in unaffiliated unions jumped from 250,000 to 625,000.

Some of these smaller unions were able to carry real clout. Like Richard Davis, Joseph P. McDonnell, a Paterson, New Jersey, trade union leader and newspaper editor, was a grass-roots organizer. McDonnell headed the Federation of Organized Trades and Labor Unions of the State of New Jersey Legislative Committee between 1883 and 1897. It wasn't a very large union, but it was an effective one. Every year, the committee reviewed labor conditions, drew up laws, and pressed legislators for change.

By 1880 New Jersey was the eighth-largest industrial state. Paterson had thriving businesses, mostly silk and textile factories. But there were other trades as well, including locomotive and machine shops. Between 1885 and 1893 McDonnell's group initiated eight significant factory laws. They included mandates for fire escapes and adequate ventilation, limits on the number of children that could be hired for dangerous work, and seats and private areas for women so that they could change into their work clothes in privacy. A big gain was the adoption of a 55-hour workweek for factory workers; New Jersey became the first state to have such legislation.

There's no disputing that McDonnell was a tireless, fiery leader—as the *Boston Post* wrote in 1897, "Every labor law on the state statute books of New Jersey owes its birth to the fostering care and indefatigable work of McDonnell"—but the community had a lot to do with his

When George Pullman (shown here) cut their wages, employees at his Pullman Palace Car Company struck. A boycott of Pullman cars soon led to a general railroad strike, and federal troops were deployed to keep the trains running.

Uncle Sam steps in to settle a railroad strike. When the government intervened in labor disputes, its actions usually helped management and hurt labor.

union's hard-won successes. What Paterson had going for it was several industries as well as residents who fought for their rights and united for the common good. As far back as 1880, when the owner of a large mosquito netting mill threatened to move his operation in retaliation against striking workers, supporters collected strike funds (money to help striking workers pay their bills until they went back to work) and circulated petitions at recreational gatherings and picnics. Other textile mills in the area also hired some of the strikers. When the owner tried another strategy—recruiting out-of-state workers—2,000 townspeople and workers met them at the train depot, harassing them and offering to pay their return fare. After nine months of haggling, the mill owner gave up.

A unified front, like the one put up in Paterson, ultimately gave America's labor unions the strength they needed to survive and grow.

FURTHER READING

Barck, Oscar Theodore, Jr., and Nelson Manfred Blake.
Since 1900: A History of the United States in Our Times.
New York: Macmillan Publishing Co., 1974.

Birmingham, Stephen. *Certain People: America's Black Elite.*
Boston: Little Brown & Co., 1977.

Brown, Ezra, ed. *This Fabulous Century — America 1870–1900 — Nation on the Move.* New York: Time-Life Books, Inc., 1985.

Brinkley, Alan, et al. *American History: A Survey. Vol. 2, Since 1865.*
New York: McGraw-Hill, Inc., 1991.

Clark, Judith Freeman. *America's Gilded Age: An Eyewitness History.*
New York: Facts On File, 1992.

Claypool, Jane. *The Worker in America — Issues in American History.* New York: Franklin Watts, 1985.

Evans, Sara M. *Born for Liberty: A History of Women in America.* New York: The Free Press, 1989.

Flatow, Ira. *They All Laughed . . . From Light Bulbs to Lasers: The Fascinating Stories Behind the Great Inventions that Have Changed Our Lives.* New York: HarperCollins, 1992.

Gutman, Herbert G. *Work, Culture & Society in Industrializing America.* New York: Alfred A. Knopf, 1976.

Katz, William Loren, and Jacqueline Hunt Katz. *Making Our Way: America at the Turn of the Century in the Words of the Poor and Powerless.* New York: The Dial Press, 1975.

Kaplan, Daile. *Lewis Hine in Europe: The Lost Photographs.* New York: Abbeville Press Publishers, 1988.

Livesay, Harold C. *Andrew Carnegie and the Rise of Big Business.* New York: Harper Collins, 1975.

Macdonald, Anne L. *Feminine Ingenuity: Women and Invention in America.* New York: Ballantine Books, 1992.

Shapiro, Max. *The Penniless Billionaires.* New York: Times Books, 1980.

INDEX

PICTURE CREDITS

Every effort has been made to contact the copyright owners of photographs and illustrations used in this book. In the event that the holder of a copyright has not heard from us, he or she should contact Chelsea House Publishers.

LINDA LEUZZI is an author and journalist whose work has been featured in *New York Newsday, Family Circle, Ladies' Home Journal, Weight Watchers, New Woman*, and *The Norton Environmental Reader*, a college textbook. She is a consultant for the Science Museum of Long Island, an interactive science activity center for children and adults in Plandome, New York.

It is the only practicable and perfect Driving Lamp ever made. It will not blow out or jar out. It gives a clear, white light. It looks like a locomotive headlight. It throws all the light ...ht ahead from 200 to 300 feet. It burns kerosene. ...means of a spring on the back, the lamp can be ...tly placed on the front of dash. By means of a ..., which we furnish with each lamp, it can be ...ed to either side of the dash. It can also be ... on the bracket of a carriage. 11 inches high; ...es in diameter; weight, 2½ lbs.

19366. Price, each, japanned............$2.40
19367. Price, each, nickel plated..........3.20

Tubular "Search Light."

19382. This has No. 2 ...r, 1-inch wick ...akes No. O ... It will not ...out in the ...est wind and ...lly good for ... use. It has ...tin reflector ...inches in di- ...and 7 inches ...hich spreads ...ght over a ...urface. It is ...le for mills, ...houses, work ...stables, sum- ...esorts, or in ... any place ...a good light ...ired. Makes ...cellent "jack ..." for hunting or fishing at night. Price, ...$2.00

...etz Tubular Hunting Lamp."

No. 19384. Looks like a locomotive headlight. It will not blow or jar out.

The hood over the front works perfectly and without noise. When the hood is down no light escapes.

It will throw a powerful light 200 feet.

It burns kerosene oil, and will burn ten hours without refilling, 11 inches high; 6 inches in diameter; weight, 2½ lbs.

It is compact and handsome. Has a bail and can be used as a hand and wall lantern in camp. Gives a brilliant light and is absolutely safe. Price...............$3.40

Dark or Police Lanterns.

Burns Sperm Oil.

strong light and the draft is so arranged that the flame will not smoke or blow out in high winds, nor jar out in passing over rough roads. Packed complete with attachments to fit to engine. Price, each.................$9.00

New Improved Square Tubular Lamp.

No. 19395. This lamp gives a very bright light, equal to the best gas jet, and will not smoke or blow out in strongest wind; especially adapted for use in warehouses, packing houses, saw mills, lumber yards, freight yards, or in ... ...inches ....wick. Has an 8-inch silvered glass reflector. Weight, boxed, 22 lbs. Price, each...............$4.45

No. 19396. Same as No. 19385, but is smaller. Measures 16¾ inches high, 8¾ inches wide and 7½ inches deep; takes No. 2 burner and 1-inch wick. Price, each...............$3.75

STREET LAMPS.
Globe Tubular Street Lamp.
Patented.

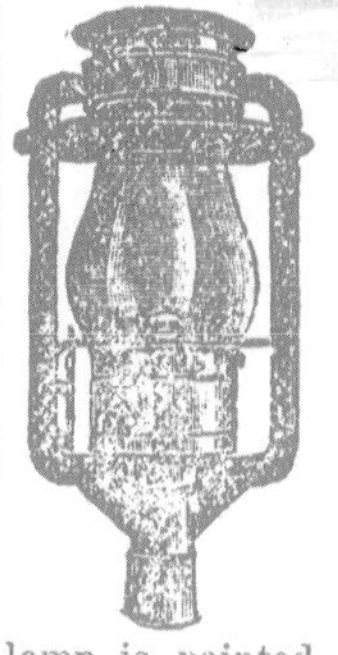

No. 19399. No. 3 burner, 1½ inch wick, No. 8 globe. Warranted to give perfect satisfaction; more sold than all other makes combined; no chimney; light equal to gas at a less cost; new globe lifter; outside wick regulator; does not smoke; casts no shadow; will not blow out in the strongest wind; can be regulated to burn a certain number of hours.

This lamp never fails to give perfect satisfaction. It can be filled, lighted and regulated without removing the globe. The reflector is painted white and the lamp is painted green. With our iron bracket it makes a useful and ornamental fixture. Packed 1 in a case. Average weight, with case, 30 lbs. Each..................$4.10

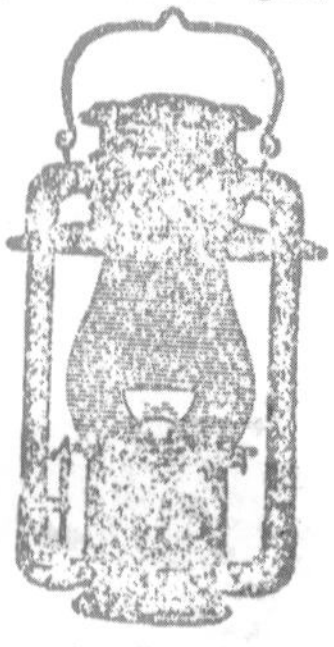

No. 19400. Globe Tubular Hanging Lamp is the same as our globe street lamp, but is intended to hang by the bail instead of fitting on post. It will be found very convenient, as it can be moved from time to time as occasion requires. Each $3.75

No. 19405. Genuine Improved Rochester Tubular Central Draft Street Lamp. Made of the best material in a substantial manner, it will give more light than any other street lamp made, and requires less attention. Particularly adapted for use at approaches to residences, on drive-ways, piers, landing stages, public streets, or any place where a good, clear and reliable light is desired. They come packed one in a box, and can be shipped any distance without danger of breaking. Price...................$4.95

No. 19407. Genuine improved Rochester Tubular Central Draft Street Lamp, constructed on same principle as No. 19405, but is to be hung by the bail

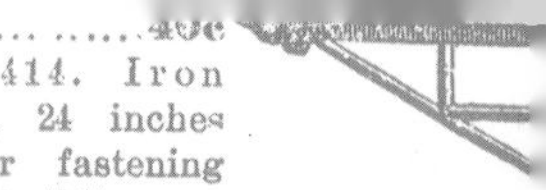

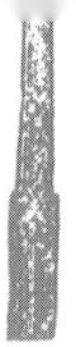

No. 19414. Iron Brackets, 24 inches long, for fastening lamp to buildings or posts. Price, each....$1.00

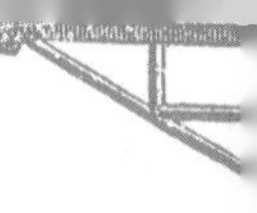

WOODENWARE DEPART...
Cedar Ware, with Elect...
Welded Hoops—Galvani...

No wood known to man will resis... equal to Virginia white cedar.

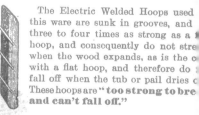

The Electric Welded Hoops used ... this ware are sunk in grooves, and ... three to four times as strong as a ... hoop, and consequently do not stre... when the wood expands, as is the c... with a flat hoop, and therefore do ... fall off when the tub or pail dries ... These hoops are "too strong to bre... and can't fall off."

Cedar Tubs.
With Electric Welded Hoop...

Made from the best Virginia white cedar. T... have met with wonderful success among our ... tomers. They ... still very st... durable, and ... ed with the ... and paint. ... guaranteed n... "fall down." ...

Those fami... the lasting ... of cedar shi... posts will a... the value of ... terial when ...

No. 16700.

tubs and pails. We have four sizes. No. 16700.

Size, No.	Diameter at Top.	Diameter at Bottom.	Depth.	Holds Gallons
0	23⅞	21⅜	12⅝	21
1	22⅜	19	11¹⁄₁₆	16
2	20⅝	17⅝	10¾	13
3	18½	16⅜	9⅛	9½

Sizes given above are inside measurements.

Cedar Water Pails.
With Galvanized Electric Welded

These pails have proven greatest selling article we ... put on the market.

They are impervious t... very light and strong, and ... way superior to any pail ev... Made of the best Virgin... cedar.

No. 16705. Two-Hoop Ce... painted with the purest ... lead and oil on the outside ... eter inside of top, 11¼ ... diameter inside of bot... inches; depth inside, 8 inches; holds 2¾ gal... each; 15c.; per doz.

No. 16706. Three-Hoop Cedar Pails, painted ... purest best lead and oil on the outside, ... inside of top, 11⅜ inches; diameter inside bo... inches; depth, 9⅜ inches; holds 3¼ gals. Pr... 18; per doz.

No. 16707. Three-Hoop Cedar Pail, made of ... selected Virginia white cedar, and finished in ... wood. Nickel plated electric welded hoop, ... finished; a very handsome pail. Diameter in ... 11¼ inches; diameter inside bottom, 8⅜ inch... inside, 8 inches; holds 2¾ gals. Price...